A LOOK AT EARTH SCIENCE

ENVIRONMENTAL SCIENCE

BY MARTIN HARASYMIW

Gareth Stevens
PUBLISHING

Please visit our website, www.garethstevens.com. For a free color catalog of all our high-quality books, call toll free 1-800-542-2595 or fax 1-877-542-2596.

Library of Congress Cataloging-in-Publication Data

Names: Harasymiw, Martin, 1978- author.
Title: Environmental science / Martin Harasymiw.
Description: Buffalo : Gareth Stevens Publishing, 2025. | Series: A look at earth science | Includes index. | Audience: Grades 4-6
Identifiers: LCCN 2024008115 (print) | LCCN 2024008116 (ebook) | ISBN 9781482467185 (library binding) | ISBN 9781482467178 (paperback) | ISBN 9781482467192 (ebook)
Subjects: LCSH: Environmental sciences–Juvenile literature.
Classification: LCC GE115 .H37 2025 (print) | LCC GE115 (ebook) | DDC 550–dc23/eng/20240314
LC record available at https://lccn.loc.gov/2024008115
LC ebook record available at https://lccn.loc.gov/2024008116

First Edition

Published in 2025 by
Gareth Stevens Publishing
2544 Clinton Street
Buffalo, NY 14224

Copyright © 2025 Gareth Stevens Publishing

Designer: Jennifer Schoembs
Editor: Therese M. Shea

Photo credits: Cover, p. 1 PopTika/Shutterstock.com; series art (backgrounds) Olena Boronchuk/Shutterstock.com; p. 5 Mike Pellinni/Shutterstock.com; p. 7 Evgeny Haritonov/Shutterstock.com; p. 9 LEDOMSTOCK/Shutterstock.com; p. 11 Maryshot/Shutterstock.com; p. 13 SERDTHONGCHAI/Shutterstock.com; p. 15 Patrizio Martorana/Shutterstock.com; p. 17 niderlander/Shutterstock.com; p. 19 Alan Budman/Shutterstock.com; p. 21 Lena_viridis/Shutterstock.com; p. 23 (both) 2j architecture/Shutterstock.com; p. 25 Chatchawal Phumkaew/Shutterstock.com; p. 27 Sumit buranarothtrakul/Shutterstock.com; p. 29 bluedog studio/Shutterstock.com; p. 30 (icons) Kapreski/Shutterstock.com; p. 30 (icons) supanut piyakanont/Shutterstock.com.

All rights reserved. No part of this book may be reproduced in any form without permission in writing from the publisher, except by a reviewer.

Printed in the United States of America

Some of the images in this book illustrate individuals who are models. The depictions do not imply actual situations or events.

CPSIA compliance information: Batch #CS25GS: For further information contact Gareth Stevens at 1-800-542-2595.

CONTENTS

A Wide Science 4
Narrowing the Field 6
Not Only a Study 10
Problem Solvers 12
In the Field 14
In the Lab 16
Getting Results 18
With the Wildlife 20
On the Ocean 22
Where They Work 24
So Much More 28
Key Environmental Concerns 30
Glossary 31
For More Information 32
Index 32

Words in the glossary appear in **bold** type the first time they are used in the text.

A WIDE SCIENCE

The environment is everything around an organism, or living thing. It's also all the things that can affect an organism's growth, health, and **survival**. Those who study the environment are called environmental scientists. They study Earth, its **processes**, and its plants and animals.

MAKE THE GRADE: The environment includes things we can see and can't see, including soil, water, and air.

NARROWING THE FIELD

Environmental science covers many, many fields of science. Biology is one of the main ones. It's the study of organisms and life processes. Ecology is the study of how organisms **interact** with the environment. Meteorology is the study of Earth's **atmosphere** and weather.

MAKE THE GRADE

Geology is the study of the history of Earth. Environmental scientists called geologists learn a lot from studying rocks that formed long ago.

Environmental science covers so much that scientists often choose one field to study closely. For example, they might choose a kind of biology called botany. This is the study of plants. Even that is a wide subject. So, a scientist might study one endangered plant.

MAKE THE GRADE

"Endangered" means in danger of dying out. As many as two out of every five plants on Earth are endangered.

NOT ONLY A STUDY

Most environmental scientists **focus** on a certain part of the natural world and try to understand how people affect it. Then, they work to preserve, or save, that part of the environment from harmful human activities, such as **polluting** and overfishing.

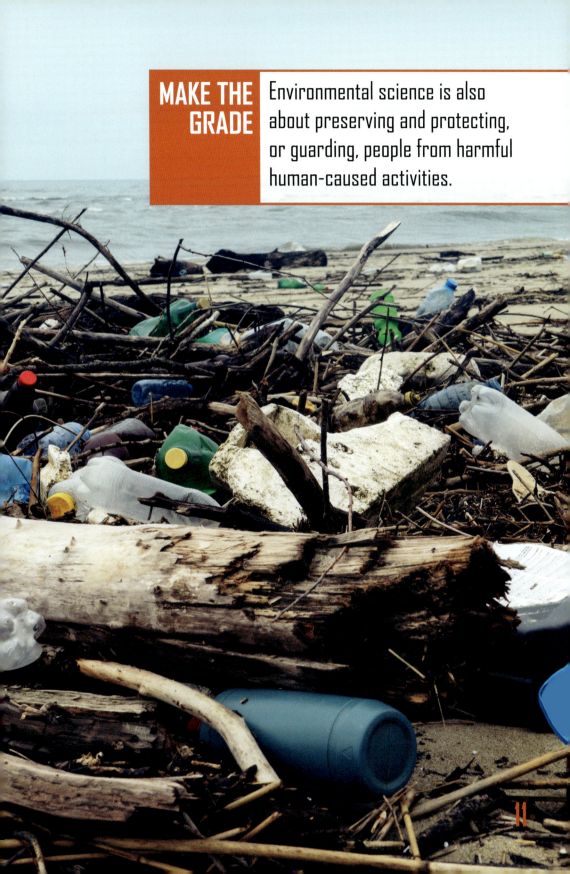

MAKE THE GRADE | Environmental science is also about preserving and protecting, or guarding, people from harmful human-caused activities.

PROBLEM SOLVERS

Environmental scientists use their knowledge of the natural world to suggest solutions, or answers, to problems. Some environmental problems today are global warming, which is the rise of Earth's **average surface temperature,** and deforestation, which is the clearing of forests.

MAKE THE GRADE

Deforestation and global warming are connected. When trees are cut down, they release, or let go, the gas carbon dioxide into the atmosphere. Carbon dioxide is one of the gases that traps heat on Earth.

IN THE FIELD

How do environmental scientists learn about the environment? They go into the field! That means going into nature to study what's going on. They may spend a lot of time watching animals. They may gather samples, or small bits, of soils, rocks, water, air, or plants.

MAKE THE GRADE

Environmental scientists may focus on one small part of the environment. However, they need to know about many kinds of science to fully understand what's happening to an organism or **habitat**.

IN THE LAB

Environmental scientists may bring their samples back to an office or lab to study them. This is where a knowledge of **chemistry** helps. For example, a scientist may study polluted water to see what kind of chemicals are present in it.

MAKE THE GRADE Environmental scientists who study water are sometimes called water **quality** scientists or water pollution scientists.

GETTING RESULTS

Finding out something is wrong is just the start. If there's a problem in the environment, the scientist will try to figure out why. They also figure out who or what is in danger. They may suggest an action to stop further harm from happening.

MAKE THE GRADE
Some environmental scientists study air quality. Air pollution can cause many health problems.

WITH THE WILDLIFE

Some environmental scientists, called wildlife biologists, work with wild animals. They may focus on a species and spend time in its habitat. If the species is in trouble, they suggest how to improve, or better, the habitat. They may suggest moving a population for its survival.

MAKE THE GRADE Wildlife biologists might use **technology** such as trail cameras to help with their studies.

ON THE OCEAN

Some environmental scientists study the ocean and what's in it. This is called oceanography. Oceans cover almost three-fourths of Earth's surface. They're home to more than 200,000 known animal and plant species. Scientists think as many as 2 million ocean species haven't been discovered yet!

MAKE THE GRADE

Some scientists study the chemistry of ocean water. Others study the water's movement. Oceans **currents** help make Earth's weather less extreme, or wild.

WHERE THEY WORK

In the United States, many environmental scientists work for the federal, or national, government. The Environmental Protection Agency (EPA) is a part of the U.S. federal government. Its job is to protect human health and the environment. Most U.S. environmental scientists work for state governments.

MAKE THE GRADE — Canada's environmental protection agency is called Environment and Climate Change Canada.

Environmental scientists work for businesses too. Many businesses need to make sure they don't harm the environment with their products or processes. For example, environmental scientists can help the businesses track chemicals they use so the chemicals don't end up in the water supply.

MAKE THE GRADE Mining companies hire many environmental scientists. That's becaue their work alters, or changes, Earth itself.

27

SO MUCH MORE

There's a growing need for people around the world to study environmental science. Do you have an interest in the natural world? Do you want to make our world better and safer for everyone? Environmental science might hold the job for you!

MAKE THE GRADE In 2022, about 80,500 environmental scientists were working in the United States. The number needed is expected to rise by about 4,000 by 2031.

KEY ENVIRONMENTAL CONCERNS

 air pollution

 land pollution

 water pollution

 the use of plastics

 global warming

 deforestation

 endangered animals and plants

 rising human population

 too much waste

GLOSSARY

average surface temperature: The average temperature over sea and land. The average is figured out by finding the sum of temperatures and dividing it by the total number of temperatures.

atmosphere: The mixture of gases that surround a planet.

chemistry: The study of chemicals, or matter that mixes with other matter to cause changes.

current: A movement of water in one direction.

focus: To direct your attention or effort to something specific.

habitat: The natural place where an animal or plant lives.

interact: To meet and have an effect on each other.

pollute: To make something dirty and not safe to use.

process: A series of steps or actions to complete something.

quality: The standard or grade of something.

survival: The act of staying alive.

technology: Using science, engineering, and other industries to invent useful tools or to solve problems. Also, a machine, piece of equipment, or method created by technology.

FOR MORE INFORMATION

Books

Guy, Cylita. *Chasing Bats and Tracking Rats: Urban Ecology, Community Science, and How We Share Our Cities.* Toronto, Ontario, Canada: Annick Press, 2021.

Martineau, Susan, and Vicky Barker. *STEM Green Science at Home: Fun Environmental Science Projects to Help Kids Save the Earth.* New York, NY: Racehorse for Young Readers, 2021.

Website

The Environment: Overview
www.ducksters.com/science/environment/
Learn more about the parts of the environment and environmental issues.

Publisher's note to educators and parents: Our editors have carefully reviewed these websites to ensure that they are suitable for students. Many websites change frequently, however, and we cannot guarantee that a site's future contents will continue to meet our high standards of quality and educational value. Be advised that students should be closely supervised whenever they access the internet.

INDEX

air, 5, 14, 19
animals, 4, 14, 20, 22
biology, 6, 8
botany, 8
chemicals, 16, 23, 26
deforestation, 12, 13
ecology, 6
endangered species, 8, 9

Environmental Protection Agency (EPA), 24
geology, 7
global warming, 12, 13
government, 24, 25
health, 4, 19, 24
meteorology, 6
oceans, 22, 23

plants, 4, 8, 14, 22
pollution, 10, 16, 17, 19
rocks, 7, 14
soil, 5, 14
water, 5, 14, 17, 26
weather, 6, 23